Copyright STEMTaught. All rights reserved. No part of this publication may by reproduced or distributed in any form, by any means, graphic, electronic, or mechanical, including photocopying, taping, and recording, or posting electronically in any location, any database or memory device without the prior written consent from STEMTaught.

Subscribing STEMTaught schools and teachers may reproduce and distribute STEMTaught material for use with their students.

The Next Generation Science Standards (NGSS) are reproduced with permission from the Department of Education.

Earth's Water can be Solid or Liquid: This Ice is Nice!

Student Edition
ISBN 978-1-952346-52-1

2-ESS2-3 Earth's Systems: Obtain information to identify where water is found on Earth and that it can be solid or liquid.

Lesson Anchor

Where do we find ice on Earth?

Explore the Phenomenon!

In some places on Earth, it is so cold all the time that the ice never melts. Where do we find icebergs on Earth? Do you think there could be icebergs at the bottom of the ocean? Why do you know?

We find lots of ice in the coldest places on Earth.

Explain the phenomenon:

Where is ice found on Earth?
Where is water found on Earth?

Explore ice and water

To understand where we find water and ice on Earth, you can observe water and ice.

What you need:

Water, ice cubes, a cup and Therma thermometer

What you will do:

Step 1: Make a prediction. Do you think your ice will sink or float in water?

Step 2: Experiment with Ice and water to test your prediction. Do your ice cubes sink or float?

Step 3: Measure the temperature of your water before and after you add ice.

before	after

Think, Pair, Share!

What can you learn from your ice exploration to help explain where ice is found on Earth?

What do you see around you?

To see where water and ice are found on Earth, wouldn't it be nice to look down from high above? What would your school, home or neighborhood look like from a bird's eye view?

This hawk views the Earth with a bird's eye view, meaning that it looks at the ground from above.

What would you see from above like a bird?

Looking down from above

What if you were a bird, looking down from high above? You would see the tops of peoples' heads. You might see black hair, blonde hair, auburn hair, red hair or no hair! You might see interesting hats and headbands. You would see the tops of houses, as well as streets and trees.

Draw what your neighborhood would look like from a bird's eye view.

What if you could fly higher than a bird?

What if you could see the Earth from space? What would it look like to see the entire planet?

This photo of Earth is taken from the International Space Station. This is what an astronaut sees.

Think, Pair, Share! Describe what you notice about the Earth. What can you see?

Looking down from above

The Earth is really a very special planet. Here's what some astronauts have written about seeing the Earth from far away. A bird's eye view (or astronaut's view) helps us to see Earth's beauty.

Aleksei Leonov - Astronaut (USSR)

Alexsei was the first man to leave his capsule for a spacewalk. He said;

"The Earth was small, light blue, and so touchingly alone."

Astronaut Edgar Mitchell (USA), described what it was like to watch the earthrise from the surface of the moon.

"Suddenly, from behind the rim of the moon, there emerged a sparkling blue and white jewel, laced with swirling white clouds, rising like a small pearl in a sea of black mystery. It takes more than a moment to fully realize that this is Earth, our home."

Astronaut Edgar Mitchell walks on the surface of the moon.

Colors can cause feelings

These astronauts described the colors that they saw. Colors can make people feel a certain way or think of certain things. How colors make us feel has been studied a lot. Your favorite restaurant might be painted red, because that makes you hungrier. The color purple usually makes us feel calm and relaxed. Yellow is a cheerful color—unless you're a baby, in which case, it might make you cry!

Think, Pair, Share!

Can you see the colors green, blue, and orange in this photo? How do these colors make you feel?

Write down or draw how these colors make you feel.

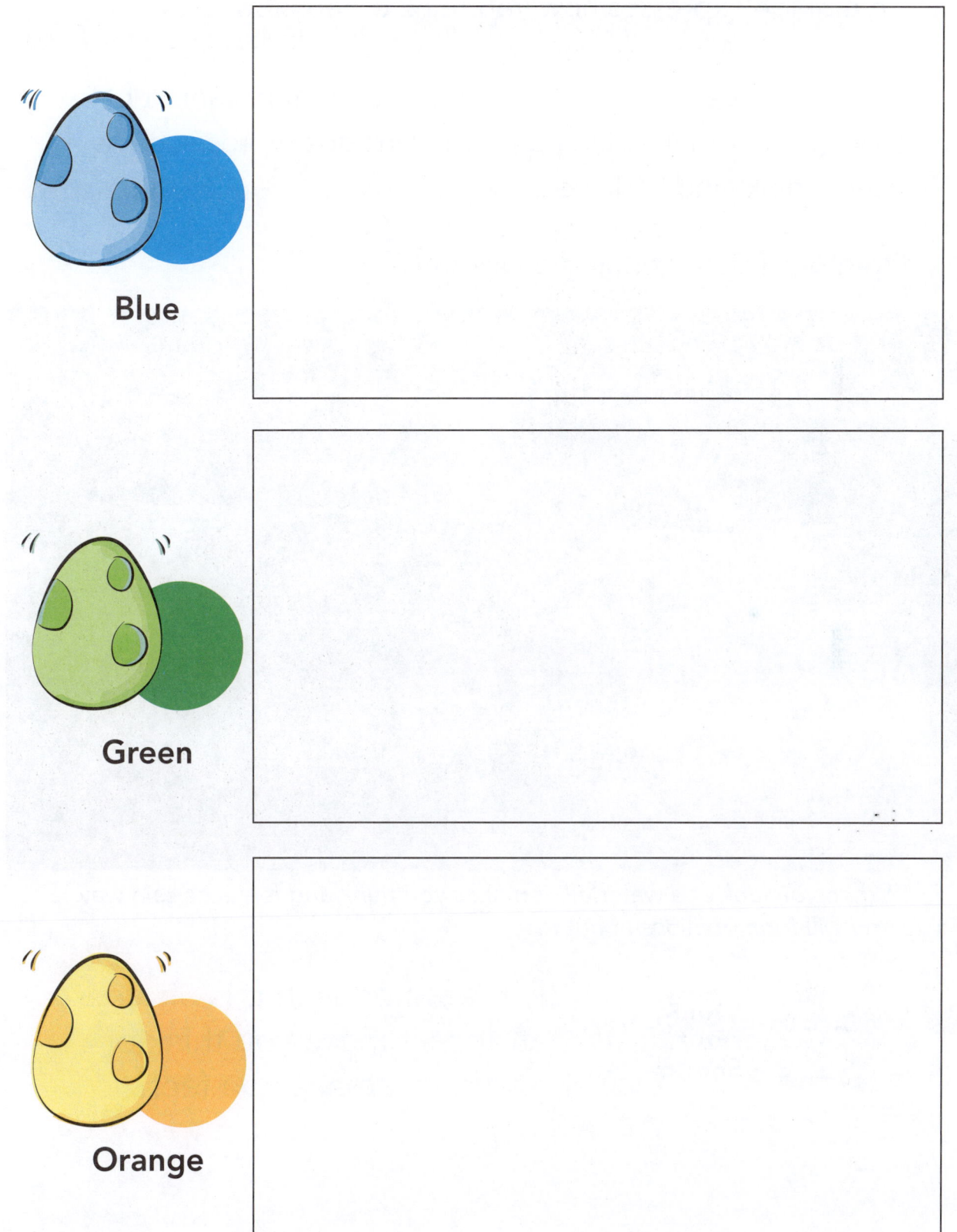

An opinion expresses your feelings

An opinion expresses how you think or feel about something. When you recorded how each color made you feel, these were your opinions. An opinion cannot be proven true or false. Opinions may include words such as 'feel', 'think' and 'believe'.

Opinion: This waterfall is awesome.

When you look at a waterfall, it makes you think and feel a certain way. You will form opinions about it.

Think, Pair, Share!

Study the waterfall in this photo. What does it make you think or how does it make you feel?

An fact can be proven to be true

A fact is a statement which can be proven to be true. You can use a measurement, scientific logic, or reasoning to show that a fact is true. It is a fact that lemons are sour. Whether or not you like that sour taste is your opinion.

Fact: This waterfall is 90 feet tall.

This is a photo of Havasu Falls taken while doing science projects with the Havasupai students.

What are some facts that you could find out about this waterfall?

These students are using Pippi pipette, Therma thermometer, and Tedros test tube to observe and describe water.

Describe water with facts and opinions

We all depend on water to live. You drink water everyday, but have you ever tried to describe water?

What you need:

- Pippi pipette
- Tedros test tube
- Therma thermometer
- A cup

What you will do:

1. Use Pippi pipette to put some water in Tedros test tube.

2. Observe, feel, taste, and measure your water.

3. Describe your water.

Draw and write: Express your opinions and state the facts about your water.

My facts about water

The height of the water in my test tube is _____ millimeters.

The temperature of my water is _____°F or _____°C.

Another fact about my water is:

_____

_____

_____

My opinions about water

I think the water is:

_____

_____

_____

I think the water feels:

_____

_____

_____

Draw some of the places you think fresh water is found.

Earth is mostly blue

Our planet is called the blue planet because it has water. Almost 72 percent of the Earth is covered with water! That is a fact. However, most of the water on Earth is salty ocean water. Drinkable freshwater can also be found in many different places on Earth.

 Think, Pair, Share!

What are some places we can find fresh water?

The Landsat 8 satellite orbits the Earth imaging all the water, ice, and land every 16 days.

We use satellites to see Earth's water

Most of Earth's fresh water is frozen. Ice is found near Earth's poles, in mountains and in glaciers. We can see Earth's water and ice with satellite photos taken from the Landsat 8 satellite. It can circle our planet in 99 minutes and it photographs the entire surface of Earth once every 16 days.

The Landsat 8 satellite's path

The Landsat 8 satellite circles the Earth high up in space. In the diagram to the left, you can see a path of photos taken on its path through the Arctic.

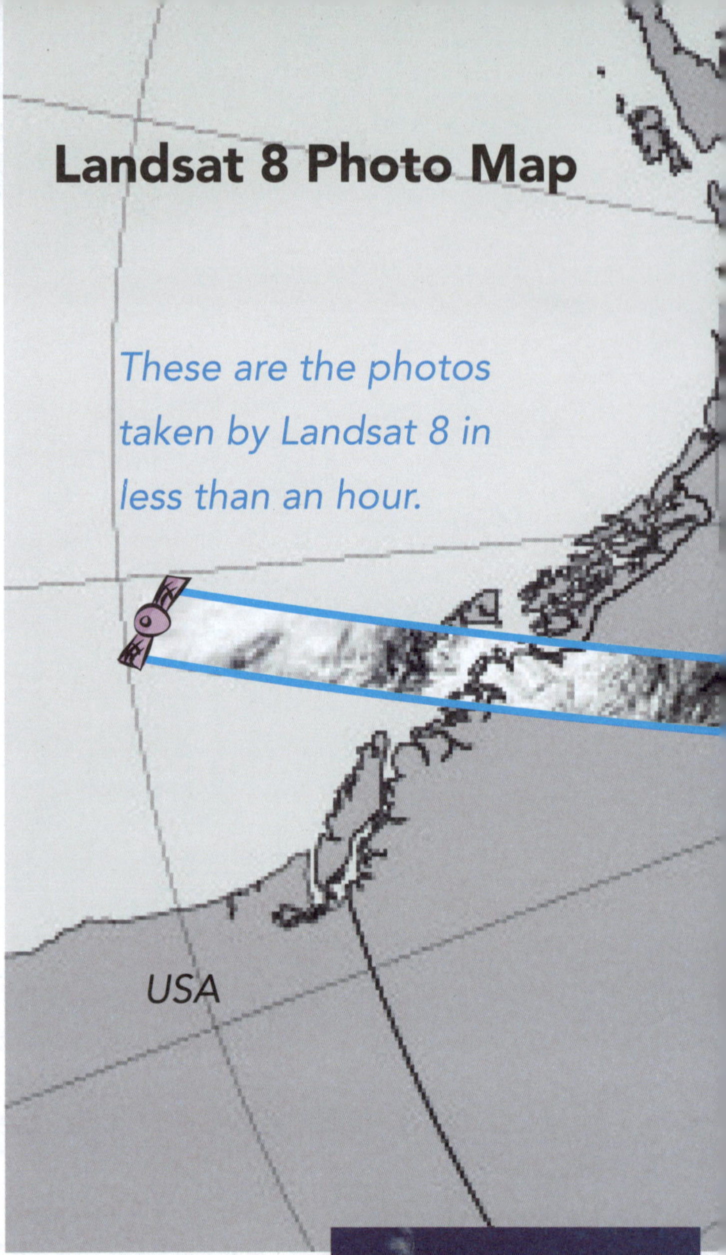

Landsat 8 Photo Map

These are the photos taken by Landsat 8 in less than an hour.

USA

First, scientists and engineers built the satellite.

Then, it was launched into space.

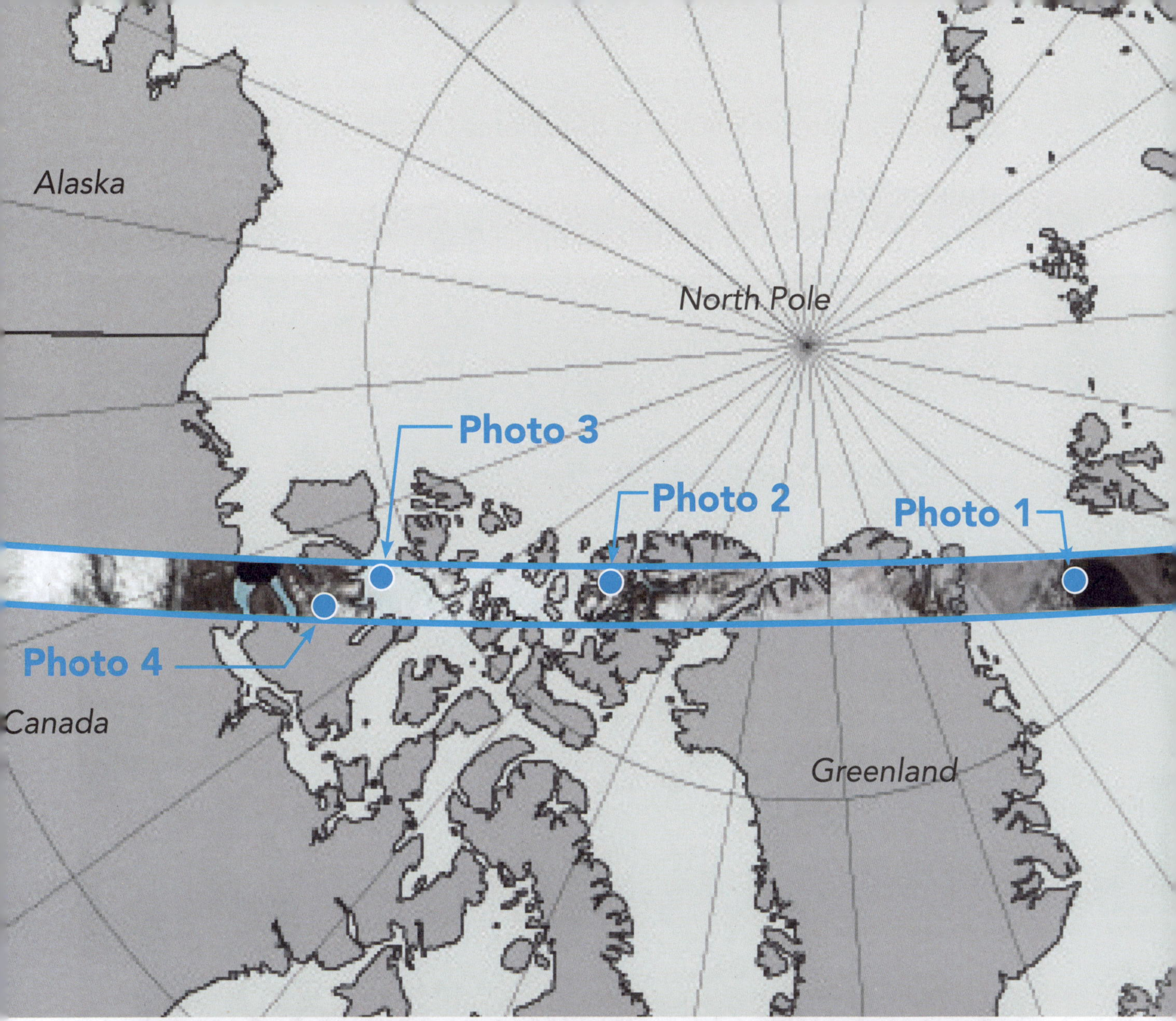

Alaska

North Pole

Photo 3

Photo 2

Photo 1

Photo 4

Canada

Greenland

Now, the satellite photographs the Earth along its orbital path.

Compare the satellite photos to the photos of each site.

Satellite View
Photo 1: Broken sea ice, Greenland Sea

Think, Pair, Share!

What do these photos teach us about Earth's water?

Satellite View
Photo 2: Glaciers and snow, Ellesmere Island, Canada

Satellite View

Think, Pair, Share!

What do these photos teach us about Earth's water?

Satellite View
Photo 3: The edge of the sea ice, Amundsen Gulf, Canada

Think, Pair, Share!

What do these photos teach us about Earth's water?

Satellite View
Photo 4: Rivers and lakes, Victoria Island, Canada

What do these photos teach us about Earth's water?

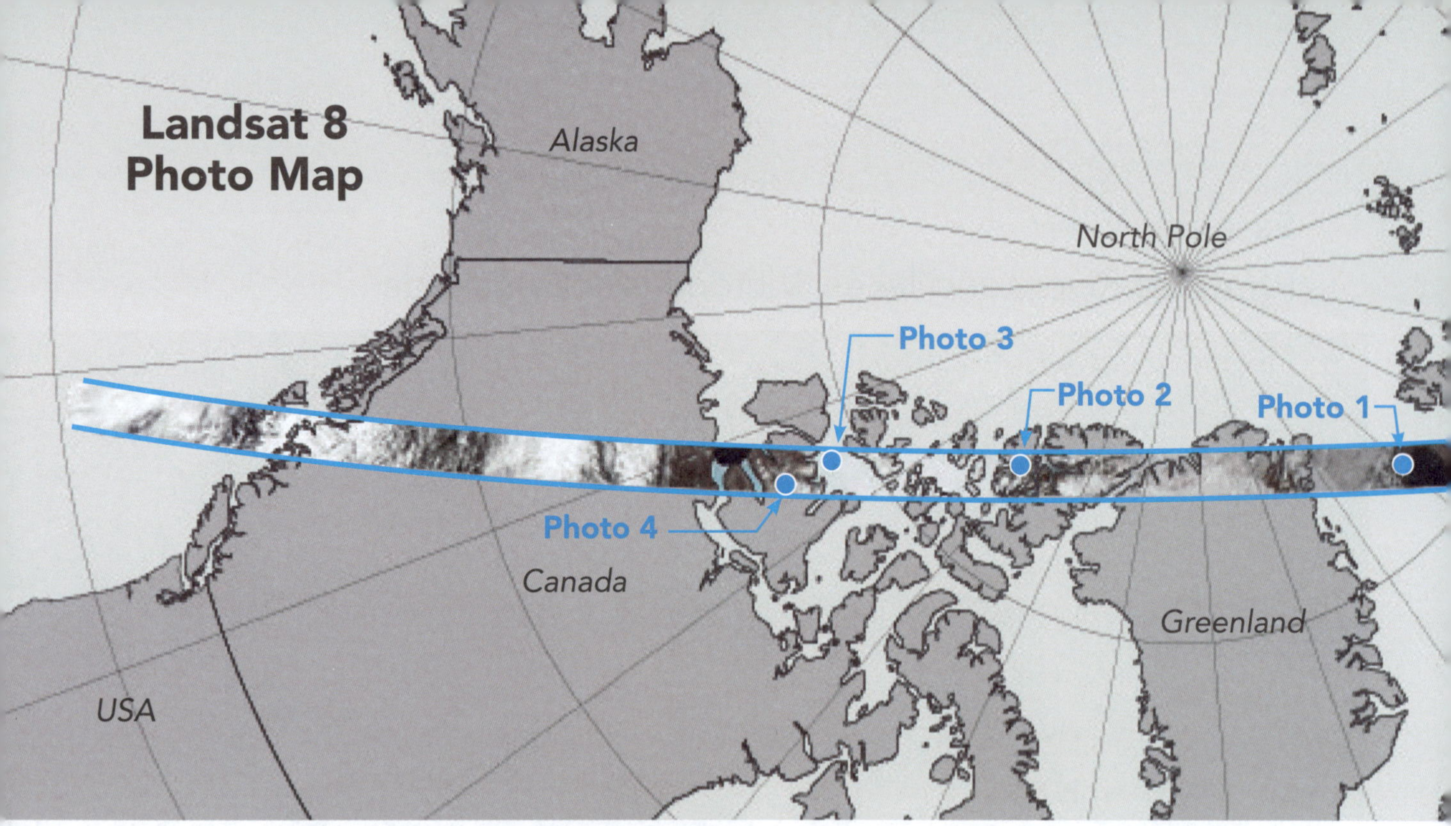

Landsat 8 Photo Map

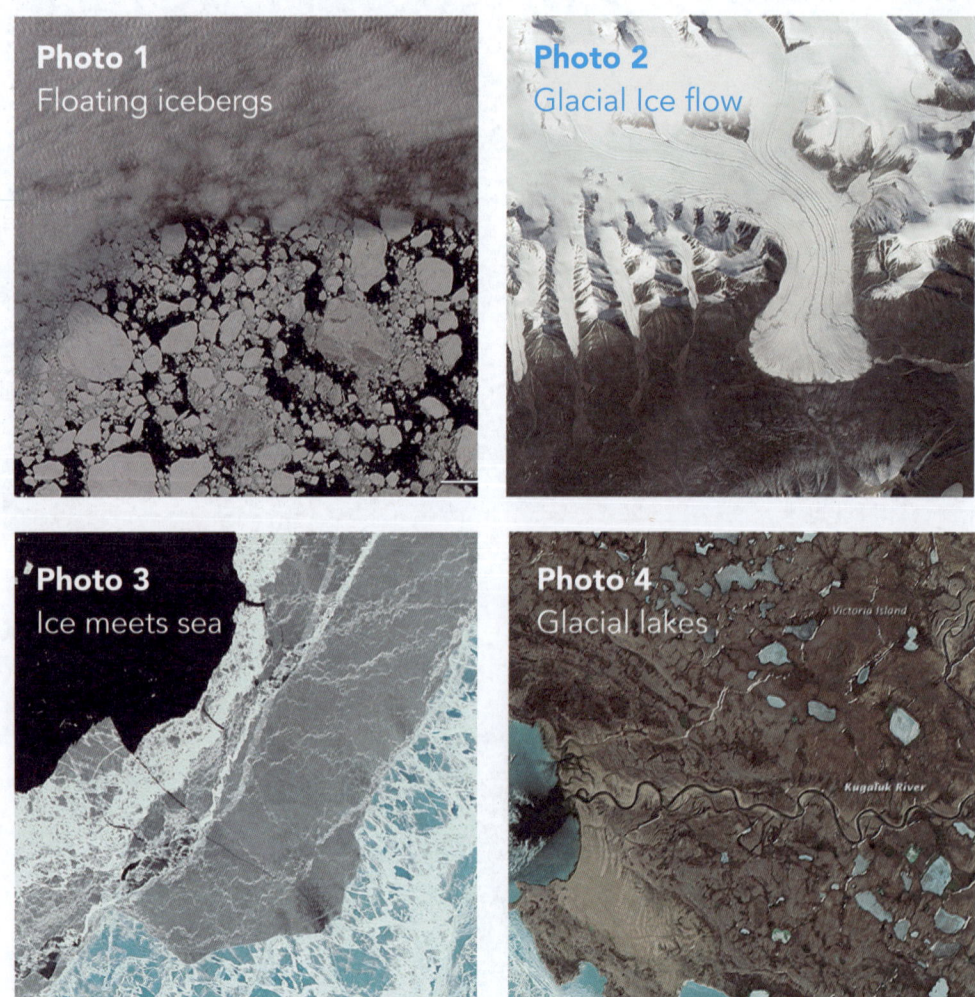

Photo 1 Floating icebergs

Photo 2 Glacial Ice flow

Photo 3 Ice meets sea

Photo 4 Glacial lakes

Earth's water is found in many places

Review the satellite images to answer the questions.

Where did you see liquid water in these photos?

_____

_____

_____

Where did you see solid water in these photos?

_____

_____

_____

What patterns did you notice about where water is found on Earth?

_____

_____

_____

Think, Pair, Share!

Where do we find fresh water on Earth?

To understand where we find fresh water and ice on Earth, it is important to observe how salt water evaporates.

Make a prediction:

What will happen when salt water is left out in open air? Will the salt evaporate with the water or will it be left behind?

_____

_____

Now experiment to test your prediction.

What you need:

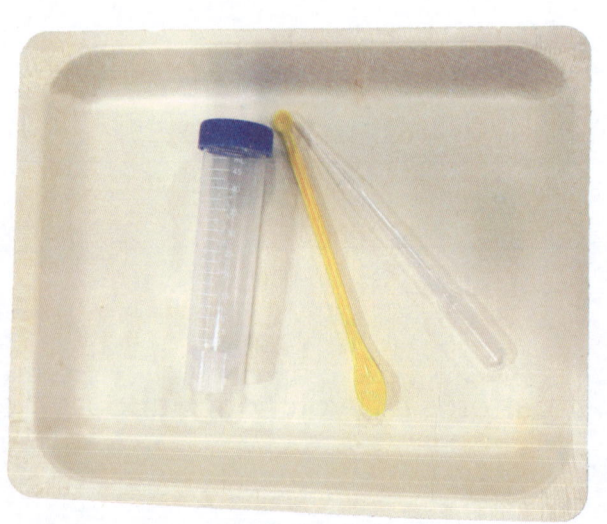

- Water

- Salt

- Pippi pipette

- Tedros test tube

- Scoopy spoon

- Petri dish (or plate)

What you will do:

1. Mix your salt water.

2. Put a few drops of salt water on a petri dish or plate.

3. Put a few drops of fresh water on a petri dish or plate.

4. Observe the area after the water evaporates.

These students are mixing salt water to test how it evaporates.

What did you notice about how salt water evaporates?

_____

_____

_____

What did you notice about how fresh water evaporates?

_____

_____

_____

 Think, Pair, Share! **What do your observations tell us about where we should be able to find fresh water on Earth?**

Ice is found at Earth's poles

The coldest places on Earth are the North Pole and the South Pole. Thick ice sheets, sea ice, glaciers and icebergs are found there. The North Pole is found in the Arctic Ocean on shifting sheets of sea ice. Antarctica (the South Pole) is a continent covered with ice that is over a thousand feet thick!

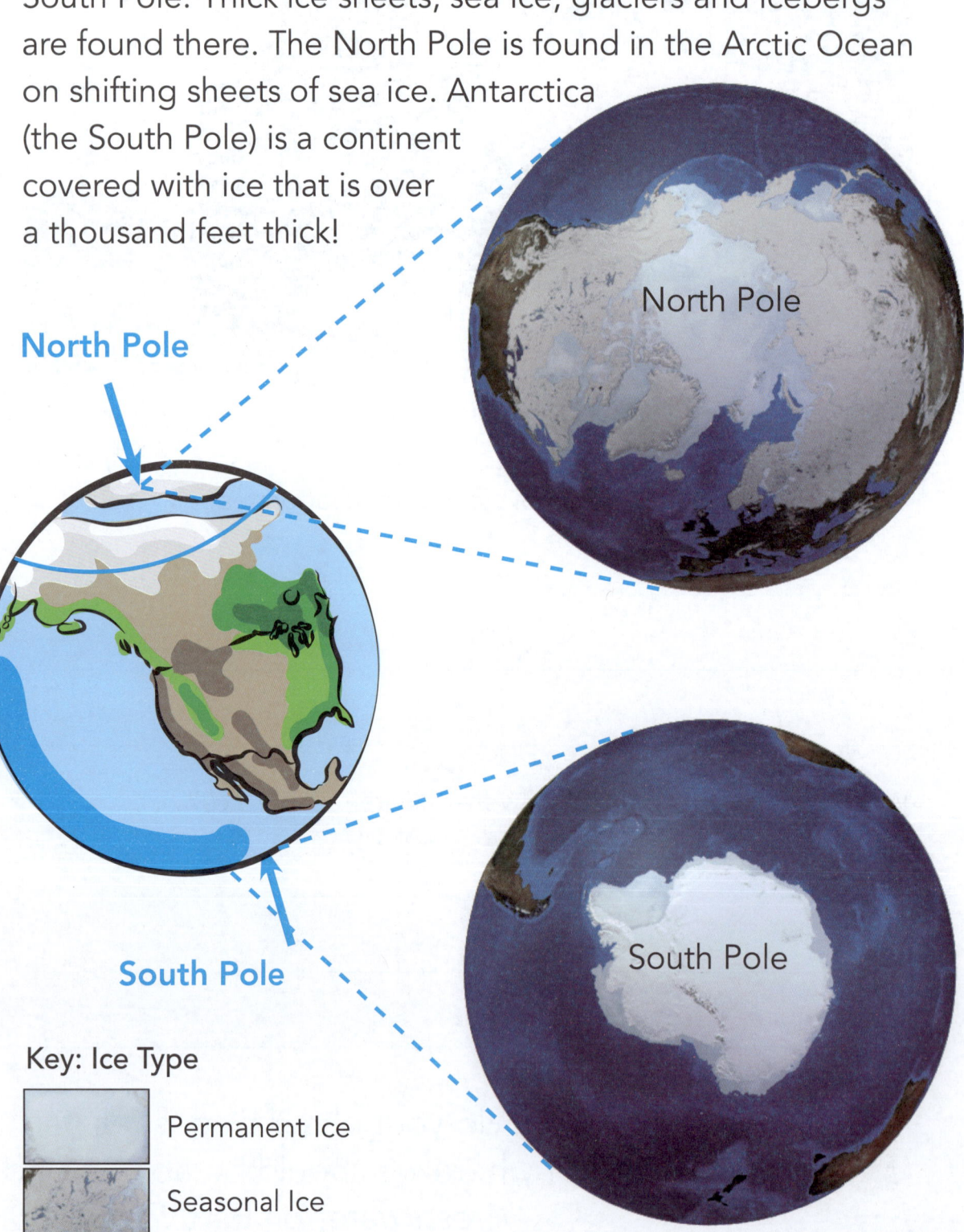

North Pole

South Pole

North Pole

South Pole

Key: Ice Type

Permanent Ice

Seasonal Ice

Fresh water is found on land

When water evaporates from the salty oceans and goes up to form clouds it leaves its salt behind. Then, it falls as fresh rain and snow. When the snow melts, it forms rivers, streams, and lakes of fresh water.

Rivers, streams, and lakes contain fresh water that we can drink.

Can you find me in the story?

The illustrations in this book feature animals found in the Arctic. As you read the story, see if you can find these animals.

Check off the animals that you find in the illustrations of the story!

Meet Qila, she is a
☐ **NARWHAL**

Meet Nanook, he is a
☐ **POLAR BEAR**

Narwhals are small whales that have a long tooth, or tusk that sticks out of their head like a unicorn horn. Narwhals do not use much energy to swim and can hold their breath a very long time.

Polar bears live and hunt for food on sheets of Arctic sea ice near the North Pole. Polar bears are dependent on the sea ice for survival. They have large, furry feet and sharp claws that help them grip the ice.

☐ ARCTIC CHAR

The Arctic char can live in saltwater and freshwater. No other freshwater fish is found as far North as the Arctic char.

☐ ARCTIC HARE

The Arctic hare is a rabbit that lives in the Arctic circle. They turn brown in the summer and white in the winter.

☐ PENGUIN

Penguins are flightless birds that are excellent swimmers. Penguins are only found in the Southern Arctic regions.

☐ JELLYFISH

The Arctic red jellyfish is the largest known jellyfish in the world. It can grow up to 7ft in diameter.

☐ ARCTIC TERN

The Arctic tern has the longest migratory routes of any animal on Earth. They travel up to 70,000 km per year.

☐ ORCA WHALE

The orca is a toothed whale that feeds on fish, seals and even other whales.

☐ ARCTIC COD

Arctic cod survive in sub-zero temperatures that would kill other fish. They have blood that prevents ice from forming.

☐ HERRING

Herring are schooling fish that live in the North Atlantic Ocean. They are an important food scource for larger animals.

Arctic animals depend on ice for survival

There are many animals that depend on Arctic ice for survival. Polar bears live and hunt for food on sheets of Arctic sea ice. Narwhals can hold their breath longer than other marine mammals such as orca whales, so they venture deep underneath ice sheets for protection and safety. Currently, our Arctic sea ice is melting at an alarming rate because of human activities. Because of human impacts, Arctic animals such as the polar bear, the narwhal, and the orca are classified as a vulnerable species.

Because summers are getting warmer in the Arctic, places that once had thick sea ice now have thin, broken and melting ice.

THIS ICE IS NICE!

Baby Qila swims underneath the Arctic ice. The ice above her glows with chilled, pearly sunlight.

"I wish I didn't have to stay close to this breathing hole," Qila said to her mother. "I want to swim through the ocean and breathe fresh Arctic air wherever I like!"

 **Where would you expect to find places covered in ice year round like this?**

Baby Nanook walks with his mother on the Arctic ice over a frozen sea.

"There is ice as far as I can see!" Nanook said to his mother. "I just want to sit on a rock and dig my claws into some soft dirt. This ice is so slippery, hard and cold!"

35

Qila looked up at her little narwhal tusk and said, "If only this ice would melt, I'd swim to the surface and hold my tusk high for everyone to see."

Qila swam as fast as she could (which wasn't very fast) and then, 'thump!' She bumped into the ice.

"Ouch!" she exclaimed. "I wish this ice would melt."

Nanook looked down at his little polar bear paws and said, "If only this ice would melt, I would use my paws to spin round and round in the nice, soft dirt."

Nanook spun round and round as gracefully as he could (which wasn't very graceful), and then, 'thump!' he slipped on the ice and fell down.

"Ouch!" he exclaimed. "I just wish this ice would melt."

Think, Pair, Share!

What types of animals do you see in the illustration that like living in the Arctic?

"The ice is a good place for us," said mother narwhal. "We sing together as we swim. When we find halibut and cod under the ice, we feast.

Qila wasn't convinced. She was quickly growing up! "I must explore the whole Arctic sea!" she exclaimed.

Think, Pair, Share!

Why is the Arctic ice a good place for a narwhal?

"The ice is a good place for us," said mother polar bear. "At night, we sit and watch the dazzling Northern Lights and we have plenty to eat."

Nanook wasn't convinced. "I'm getting quite big now! Soon, I must take care of myself," he said.

Mother bear saw that it was true. She couldn't help feeling sad, because babies are always babies for mommies, even when they are big.

Think, Pair, Share!

Why is the Arctic ice a good place for a polar bear?

Narwhals like to stick together.

"I suppose we could go to the open sea," mother narwhal cautiously said. "Just for a little while."

Qila set off with her pod, swimming as fast as she could. Although she soon grew tired, she just kept swimming. On and on. And on. And on.

All little polar bears must eventually set off alone.

"My little cub, if you think that it's time, then I suppose you should go," mother polar bear said as she wiped away a tear.

Nanook set off to find the edge of the ice.

Soon he grew tired and wanted to rest, but he just kept walking. On and on. And on. And on.

Think, Pair, Share!

Why don't Qila and Nanook like their home?

Finally, Qila reached the edge of the melting Arctic ice. When she came up to get a breath of air she found herself alone. She had been separated from her pod. Then, she heard a loud noise ...

'Cra-a-ack, Splash!'

She hoped it might be another narwhal. But it wasn't.

How could melting and broken ice be a dangerous place for a narwhal?

Think, Pair, Share!

How could melting and broken ice be a dangerous place for a polar bear?

Nanook finally reached the edge of the melting Arctic ice. He walked carefully on the thin ice, but then ...

'Cra-a-ack, Spl-a-sh!'

The ice underneath him broke and he fell into the chilly water. He thought the soft dirt he was looking for would be at the edge of the ice. But it wasn't.

Qila was scared, tired and hungry.

Suddenly, she caught a glimpse of a giant orca whale! She'd never had trouble with orcas when she lived under the protection of the thick ice.

Qila found a small piece of floating ice. She tapped on it with her tusk, hoping her mother would hear her and come to help.

Nanook was cold, tired and hungry. He was not built to swim so far.

Finally, he found a small piece of ice to climb up on. Exhausted, Nanook laid his head on the ice and tried to rest. Then, he heard a faint tapping noise.

Nanook looked toward the sound. He was very surprised at what he saw. It was a baby narwhal!

Is melting Arctic ice a problem for Arctic animals today?

"Help!" said Qila, "There are giant orca whales and if they see me here all alone, they will surely eat me!"

Ouila heard the noise of the orca pod getting closer and closer. She longed for her home in the thick Arctic ice, where she was safe and close to her pod. She started to cry.

Nanook knew what to do!

Think, Pair, Share!

What is causing our Arctic ice to melt at such an alarming rate?

Nanook jumped into the water and gave Qila a great, big, warm bear hug.

"I'm white, just like the ice!" Nanook said, hiding her behind his snowy white fur. "If I cover you, the orcas will not be able to see you."

The orca pod was right next to them. Nanook saw a huge figure emerge from the surface of the water. Its back was smooth and gray. Nanook closed his eyes and hugged Qila even tighter.

To Qila's surprise, the giant orcas swam right past them. The orcas never even saw that they were there!

Think, Pair, Share!

How does Nanook's color help him survive out on the Arctic ice?

Nanook climbed back on the ice. He was happy he could help his friend, but he was still stuck on his little piece of floating ice.

"Help" said Nanook. "I can't get back to the solid ice sheet. It's too far for me to swim!

Qila knew just what to do!

Suddenly, Nanook felt the ice begin to move! He peered over the edge and saw Qila pushing with all her might on the piece of ice. Then, he saw more narwhals joining in. Qila's pod had finally found her!

5 years later ...

Qila swims happily with her pod underneath the frozen ice. She remembers her adventure with Nanook and no longer dreams of swimming in the open sea. She knows, now, that this is the perfect place for her to live.

Nanook naps happily on the ice. He remembers his adventure with Qila and no longer dreams of digging his claws into soft dirt. He knows, now, that this is the perfect place for him to live.

They are both happy living in the frozen Arctic, where the ice is nice.

Think, Pair, Share!

Are Qila and Nanook happier on thick ice or on the open sea? Why do you think so?

Human activities cause climates to warm

Recently, scientists have become very worried about how fast the Arctic ice has started to melt. Temperatures in the Arctic are rising at least twice as fast as temperatures in the rest of the world! When humans burn fuel to make electricity and to drive cars, harmful gases are released into the air that trap the Sun's heat and cause Earth's climates to warm up.

How do humans cause Earth's climates to warm up?

Think, Pair, Share!

This is a power plant that burns coal to make electricity. Its pollution causes Earth's climates to warm.

Clean energy can solve climate change

Knowing how we affect our Earth is important for understanding how we can make a difference in slowing climate change. People are coming up with new, clean ways to make electricity without burning dirty fuels. We can make electricity from wind and sunlight. Using forms of clean energy do not cause Earth's climates to warm.

This wind turbine makes electricity using wind energy without releasing any pollution that would cause Earth's climates to warm.

How can we slow or stop climate change?

Fun-Dixie Journal Entry

 Make a drawing to support your journal entry.

Royal
STEMTaught Post

What was your favorite part of this learning unit?

_____

_____

_____

_____

_____

When you read the STEMTaught Journal and do the fun activities inside, sometimes you just want to draw and write about it!